We are chicks.

We are in the kennel with Wellington.

This chick pecks Wellington on his chin.

Peck, peck.

This chick pecks Wellington
on his cheek.
Peck, peck.

Wellington gets cross.
"Get off me. Go away," he says.

We all get off Wellington.
We all go to look for mum.

She is in the shed.

She is on the nest.

Oh no! She has laid an egg.
She will sit on it for weeks.

We all go back to Wellington.
He is a soft cuddly dog.